LOVE TO RECONCILE
The Heart of the Father

LOVE TO RECONCILE

The Heart of the Father

ANN LINDHOLM

All scripture, unless otherwise noted, is from the Fire Bible: English Standard Version (ESV), published by Hendrickson Publishers Marketing. The Holy Bible, English Standard Version (ESV) Copyright © 2001 by Crossway Bibles, a publishing ministry of Good News Publishers. Quote marks, italics and capitalization added for emphasis and clarity and dually noted.

All rights reserved. No part of this publication may be reproduced, stored in a retrieval system, or transmitted in any form or by any means—electronic, mechanical, photocopy, recording, or any other—except for brief quotations in printed reviews, without the permission of the Author or Publisher.

Ann Lindholm Copyright© 2019

Contents

Acknowledgments
Foreward
Discipline, A Love Thing 1
Nebuchadnezzer 9
A Man After God's Own Heart 17
Prodigal Return 23
Saul to Paul 27
Father Knows Best 33
Forgiveness, Not an Option 43
Reconciliation in Relationships 49
Reconciliation as a Nation 61
What Now? 69
Tools 75
Recommended Reading 82

ACKNOWLEDGEMENTS

I have attempted multiple times to write a book because I felt the Lord calling me to that, but every attempt was tattered with my imprint and rush. It was not until I entered into a sisterhood with a very dear friend and mentor of mine that probably had the most significant influence on my life as a Christian, that this book came into being. Jennifer Smallwood led a team of us in an Inner Healing and Deliverance course in the fall of 2018. After completion of that course we continued into an internship with her. In that internship is where the Lord began to show me who He really is and what His word is all about. He began to perform heart surgery on me that would change the way I do relationships. Granted, I am far from perfect or having arrived...I still have a lot of growing and maturing to do. If it was not for Jennifer's obedience to the Lord and all that He has taught her personally, this book would never have been penned. Through Jennifer the Lord began to reveal to me His heart for reconciliation and how that is at the forefront of everything. I cannot thank Jennifer enough for the priceless truth she has allowed the Lord to reveal to me through her.

Jennifer began "You are Worthy Ministries" in 2004, as she was prompted by the Lord, which focuses on personal discipleship, inner healing, and deliverance with women. She has worked with women from all backgrounds including- human trafficking, satanic ritual abuse, rape and domestic violence. She is also involved with teaching, preaching, and interceding for the Body of Christ. She and her husband, Brent, have pastored a small house church for over seven years, which has opened many doors to discipleship. Using the scriptures as their directive and Jesus as their model they focus on spiritual growth, maturing into Christlikeness. In seeing the great need all around they have been motivated to train and equip others for the work of ministry. You can view their ministry work on YouTube at "You are Worthy," Jennifer Smallwood, or on Facebook at smallwood.hope@gmail.com.

I will be forever grateful for Jennifer's dedication to the Lord and His ministry. I love you sister! Love, Ann.

I also want to thank Lauren Lockwood, my very dear sister in Christ whom our Lord has bestowed the gift of prophetic art. I have known Lauren for over three years and we do life together as we are committed to the same church body. The Lord has birthed an amazing gift in Lauren through her mind, spirit, eyes, and hands as she creates beautiful works of art as Holy Spirit leads her. She will often create art led by the Spirit during our worship sets and undoubtedly they flow with the work that God is desiring to do that particular day. Lauren has such a sweet spirit about her that allows her to minister to others in such a way that it often leads to reconciliation. Her desire for the Lord is contagious. I have asked Lauren to produce the artwork for this book as the Spirit leads her. Thank you Lauren, I love you sister!

You can find more of her art at Etsy: HammerAndPenCreative

FOREWARD
Jennifer Smallwood

Reconciliation is the heart of the good news of the gospel that has many times been overlooked by the ways of religion and even the modern church culture. Always focusing on the need for a savior, many have lost sight of the beautiful view Jesus offers those willing to accept Him as Lord. Lordship requires that an individual accepts their need for salvation but then accepts the invitation to come boldly before the throne of God into relationship with the King of Kings. Many seem to find themselves instead, stuck in the hallway along the way, seeking an ever-improved life for themselves rather than looking to the Father, the Ancient of Days. Ann Lindholm is one, having received salvation, hungers and thirsts for righteousness and desires the One who is Truth to teach and guide her in the ways of His Kingdom. In the pages to follow, she will take you on a journey of reconsidering why God sent His only begotten Son. Perhaps He came to do more than cleanse His people of sin and, actually, has always desired to bring them into a relationship of knowing Him. I encourage and challenge readers to take their time considering the heart of a God that so longs to be known that He would go to inconceivable lengths, by our human standard, to bring His people back into right relationship with Him. Salvation is a miraculous and beautiful gift, but knowing the One who is Savior is a journey that will last all of eternity for those who choose Him.

DISCIPLINE, A LOVE THING

What is the Bible really about anyway? Many will say it is a book of stories that may or may not have actually happened. Many say that it is all about the Last Days. Some will say that it is about forgiveness. Some say it is a book of laws and a list of do's and don'ts. What do you believe the Bible is about?

I believe the Bible is all about love and reconciliation. From beginning to end, the Bible shows us the amazing love of the Father and His Son. The Bible shows a beautiful picture of God's desire and will for reconciliation for all people. It is the Father's will that none should perish and all to be reconciled to Him. (2 Peter 3:8-10). If we look at the Old Testament and the history of the Israelites who consistently went astray and rejected God, time and again the Father responds with love and the hope of reconciliation. If you are familiar with the Old Testament you may be wondering how God showed love to the Israelites when He would respond with discipline or reproof. The Word shows us that discipline is birthed from a heart of love and should be received with humility and honor.

Job 5:17-18 "Behold, blessed is the one whom God reproves; therefore despise not the discipline of the Almighty. 18 For he wounds, but He binds up; He shatters, but His hands heal.

Proverbs 13:24 Whoever spares the rod hates his son, but he who loves him is diligent to discipline him.

2 Corinthians 7:9-10 As it is, I rejoice, not because you were grieved, but because you were grieved into repenting. For you felt a godly grief, so that you suffered no loss through us. 10For godly grief produces a repentance that leads to salvation without regret (emphasis added), whereas worldly grief produces death.

Hebrews 12:5-11 And have you forgotten the exhortation that addresses you as sons? "My son, do not regard lightly the discipline of the Lord, nor be weary when reproved by him. 6For the Lord disciplines the one he loves, and chastises every son whom he receives." 7It is for discipline that you have to endure. God is treating you as sons. For what son is there whom his father does not discipline? 8You are left without discipline, in which all have participated, then you are illegitimate children and not sons. 9Besides this, we have had earthly fathers who disciplined and we respected them. Shall we not much more be subject to the Father of spirits and live? [10] For they disciplined us for a short time as it seemed best to them, but he disciplines us for our good, that we may share his holiness (emphasis added). [11]For the moment all discipline seems painful rather than pleasant, but later it yields the peaceful fruit of righteousness to those who have been trained by it.

Revelation 3:19 Those whom I love, I reprove and discipline, so be zealous and repent.

Every time the Israelites went astray and started following the ways of the world or nations around them, God would warn and often reprove them if they did not heed the warnings. The warnings may have come through prophets or priests, or some times dreams or visions. He is such a loving Father that He would give warning before disciplining. But often, they did not heed the warnings so God brought discipline because He loves His children so much that He does not want to see them lost and eternally separated from Him.

We can begin as early as the beginning, Adam and Eve. It was not long after God created the first man and woman that they began straying from the Father's commandments. He first brought judgment on the serpent for deceiving Adam and Eve, cursing him to crawl on the ground for the rest of time on earth, cursing him above all other beasts and creatures. (This explains my serious disdain for snakes.) God proceeded to discipline Eve through increasing pain during the childbearing process. (Thanks a lot Eve.) Recall that this punishment extends to all women. He removed access to the garden for both of them and cursed Adam (man) to hard labor. This discipline was not brought on Adam and Eve from a heart posture of disdain or wickedness. This discipline was brought from a heart posture of love and a desire for them to be reconciled to Himself.

We see the apple does not fall far from the tree in the devastating story of Cain and Abel, Adam and Eve's sons. God also disciplined Cain for the murder of his own brother. When God sent him away Cain believed he would be killed as he wandered, but God marked him and protected him. He proceeded to conceive children with his wife. God's desire was not to dismiss Cain altogether but for Cain to repent and be reconciled to Himself through the discipline the Father carried out on Cain.

We journey next into the dreadful rejection of God by the people during Noah's days. The people had become so corrupt and wicked and their hearts had become so hardened that there was no way for them to receive the love of the Father. As you are probably aware, God brought judgment by way of a total flood devastating the entire earth. However, He did preserve and protect Noah and his family who faithfully heeded the warning of the impending doom. Noah and his family, along with some animals, survived while the rest of the world suffered death and I believe, most likely eternal separation from God. There is a point when someone can become so hardened and completely reject God that there is no way for them to receive His love, but only his discipline and judgment. (Ezekiel 18:21-23). This is a truth that many churches and pastors shy away from teaching on. This is a truth that must be understood and accepted. The account of Noah and the people's destruction can be studied in the book of Genesis.

Following are some scriptures that teach on the judgment of God and how He will eventually give someone over to their hardened heart if they continually reject Him. Please remember though, the heart of the Father is reconciliation and He is a very patient and long-suffering Father, but He is also a very just God.

Romans 1:24 Therefore God gave them up in the lusts of their hearts to impurity, to the dishonoring of their bodies among themselves, [25]because they exchanged the truth about God for a lie and worshipped and served the creature rather than the Creator, who is blessed forever! Amen. [26] For this reason God gave them up to dishonorable passions. For their women exchanged natural relations for those that are contrary to nature; [27]and the men likewise gave up natural relations with women and were consumed with passion for one another, men committing shameless acts with men and receiving in themselves the due penalty for their error. ²⁸ And since they did not see fit to acknowledge God, God gave them up to a debased mind to do what ought not to be done. ²⁹They were filled with all manner of unrighteousness, evil, covetousness, malice. They are full of envy, murder, strife, deceit, maliciousness. They are gossips ³⁰slanderers, haters of God, insolent, haughty, boastful, inventors of evil, disobedient to parents, ³¹foolish, faithless, heartless, ruthless. ³²Though they know God's righteous decree that those who practice such things deserve to die, they not only do them but give approval to those who practice them. (Spend some time studying that list of things that are deserving of death. If any repentance needs to take place I encourage you to stop reading and spend some time with the Lord right now.) (Emphasis added).

Psalm 81:11 "But my people did not listen to my voice; Israel would not submit to me. ¹² So I gave them over to their stubborn hearts, to follow their own counsels. ¹³ Oh, that my people would listen to me, that Israel would walk in my ways! ¹⁴ I would soon subdue their enemies and turn my hand against their foes. ¹⁵ Those who hate the Lord would cringe toward him, and their fate would last forever. ¹⁶ But he would feed you with the finest wheat, and with honey from the rock I would satisfy you."

I share this truth because of my desire that all would be reconciled to the Holy One, and would not be led astray by the false teachings of the world. One cannot repeatedly reject God and remain in His graces. One cannot repeatedly reject God and expect to live in eternal security with Him in His majestic Kingdom. One cannot repeatedly reject God and expect to escape the eternal lake of fire, hell and damnation. Friend, listen to the warnings and the discipline of the Father, heed them and be reconciled to Him right now, do not delay.

NEBUCHADNEZZER

Another example we can learn from is that of King Nebuchadnezzar of Babylon around the time of 605-536 B.C. I absolutely love this story not only because of the outcome, but because it shows the awesome love and heart of the Father. Babylon invaded Judah and took over its capital, Jerusalem around 605 B.C. The captivity lasted approximately 70 years. Many Israelites were taken captive into Babylon. Daniel and his three friends, Hananiah, Mishael, and Azariah (better known as Shadrach, Meshach, and Abednego) were some of those people. (Daniel was renamed Belteshazzar by King Nebuchadnezzar.) They were brought in to serve in the king's palace and to learn the way of the Chaldeans.

While many focus on the remarkable faith and steadfast loyalty of Daniel and his three friends I actually want to look at how God dealt with King Nebuchadnezzar. He was a prideful and harsh king. We also get a quick synopsis of his character from Daniel 5:18-24. This is after Daniel interpreted a mysterious writing on the wall that came from a supernatural hand not connected to a body. (Bizarre things like this still happen today!) Do you think you would repent and turn to the Lord if you witnessed this scene?

It certainly grabbed the people's attention. Here Daniel is speaking to Nebuchadnezzar's son, Belshazzar, after he became king, but the point here is to learn about Nebuchadnezzar.

¹⁸O king, the Most High God, gave Nebuchadnezzar your father kingship and greatness and glory and majesty. ¹⁹ And because of the greatness that he gave him, all peoples, nations, and languages trembled and feared before him. Whom he would, he killed, and whom he would, he kept alive; whom he would, he raised up, and whom he would, he humbled. ²⁰ But when his heart was lifted up (became arrogant and haughty) and his spirit was hardened so that he dealt proudly, he was brought down from his kingly throne, and his glory was taken from him. ²¹He was driven from among the children of mankind, and his mind was made like that of a beast, and his dwelling was with the wild donkeys. He was wet with the dew from heaven, until he knew that the Most High God rules the kingdom of mankind and sets over it whom He will. ²²And you his son, Belshazzar, have not humbled your heart, though you knew all this, ²³but you have lifted up yourself against the Lord of heaven. And the vessels of his house have been brought in before you, and you and your lords, your wives, and your concubines have drunk wine from them. And you have praised the gods of silver, gold, bronze, iron, wood, and stone, which do not see or hear or know, but the God in whose hand is

your breath, and whose are all your ways, you have not honored. (emphasis added)"

What I want you to see here is that King Nebuchadnezzar was a very arrogant and harsh king. He was not honoring God, in fact, he was serving false gods. God delivered a warning to the king via Daniel and the interpretation of the first dream. The king saw that Daniel was not only able to interpret the dream, he was able to tell the king what his dream was without the king telling him first. This softened the kings heart to recognize the favor of the Lord on Daniel. He even goes so far as to proclaim, "Truly, your God is God of gods and Lord of kings, and a revealer of mysteries, for you have been able to reveal this mystery." (3:47). So Nebuchadnezzar's heart is beginning to be softened to the truth of God.

In chapter three Nebuchadnezzar proceeds to make a golden image, perhaps in honor of the golden head described to him in the dream that represented his kingdom. Pride was still evident. A herald commanded all the people to worship the golden image that the king had set up. Whoever refused to worship the image would be thrown into a fiery furnace. Truly a remarkable story that I encourage you to read. Again, what I want to focus on though, is not the faith of Daniel's three friends (which is amazing), rather...the love of the Father and His heart for reconciliation.

When the three men, more commonly known as Shadrach, Meshach and Abednego, refused to worship the golden image or any false god, Nebuchadnezzar's pride caused him to be filled with rage and commanded that the three be thrown into the fiery furnace after turning up the heat seven times. The guards who bound them up and threw them in died by the fire immediately. What happened next was a result of the three men accepting the opportunity to partner with God in what He was doing by refusing to worship false gods and lean on Him. They had faith that God would deliver them, and even if He didn't they proclaimed that He was still God and they would only worship Him.

When Nebuchadnezzar saw that an angel joined the three men and that they were no longer bound or touched by the fire, the king stood in astonishment calling the men out, "Shadrach, Meshach, and Abednego, servants of the Most High God, come out, and come here! (Emphasis added)" After assessing the complete lack of harm done to these men he proceeds, "Blessed be the God of Shadrach, Meshach, and Abednego, who has sent his angel and delivered his servants who trusted in Him, and set aside the king's command, and yielded up their bodies rather than serve and worship any god except their own God. Therefore, I make a decree: Any people, nation, or language that speaks anything against the God of Shadrach, Meshach, and Abednego shall be torn limb from limb, and their houses laid in ruins, for there is no other god who is able to rescue in this way (emphasis added)." (3:28-29.)

The king's heart was obviously softened to the truth of who God truly is. He began to recognize that his false gods were worthless. How often have you known someone; perhaps yourself, who is in the beginning stages of realizing the truth of who God is. We see the "three steps forward, two steps back" dance playing out in their faith. They begin to make progress in recognizing God to be the only true God. Their habits and way of thinking begin to change toward God's will. Then, out of nowhere, they take several steps back and fall into previous wrong thinking. Nebuchadnezzar was no different.

He was delivered a second dream with a warning that Daniel also interpreted. In this particular dream Nebuchadnezzar was told that unless he humbled himself his kingdom was going to be taken away from him and he'd been driven to live like a beast in the wilderness.

From reading the story you get the idea that the king failed to heed the warnings of his dream and suffered the discipline that he was warned about. King Nebuchadnezzar was humbled by the Lord in that the kingdom was taken from him and he was driven into the wilderness to live like a beast in the wild. At the end of his sentence in chapter four, verse thirty-four, Nebuchadnezzar blessed the Most High God and praised and honored Him who lives forever, proclaiming, "At the end of the days I, Nebuchadnezzar, lifted my eyes to heaven, and my reason returned to me, and I blessed the Most High, and praised and honored him who lives forever (emphasis added)..." (4:34)

As Nebuchadnezzar began praising and honoring God his reason returned to him along with his kingdom and even more greatness was added to him. Nebuchadnezzar was restored. He went on to say, "Now I, Nebuchadnezzar, praise and extol and honor the King of heaven for all his works are right and his ways are just; and those who walk in pride he is able to humble. (Emphasis added)" (4:37).

Let us recap. King Nebuchadnezzar received several warnings that he needed to humble himself before the Lord and honor Him. While he showed some improvement he also experienced some failures in fully committing to the Lord. So in failing to heed the warnings God brought discipline upon him; which, in turn, humbled him since he was unwilling to humble himself. With each encounter the king softened his heart toward the Father even more so that ultimately he accepted the reproof of the Father and submitted to Him. He was restored. The Father loves us so much that He will do whatever it takes to knock down those walls that are preventing us from being restored to Him. The Father's love leads to reconciliation.

A MAN AFTER GOD'S OWN HEART

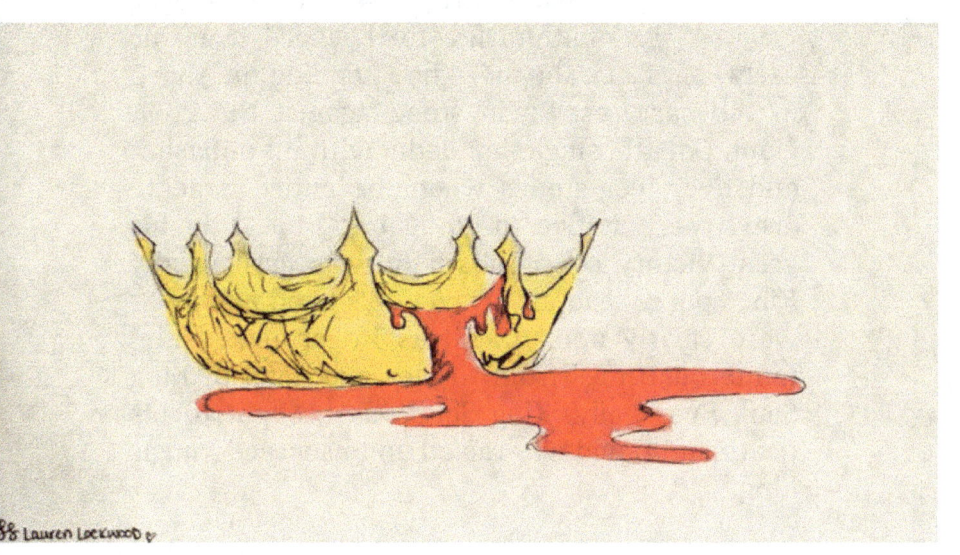

We find another amazing example of the heart of the Father in a tragic story of a man who was given the title, "A Man After God's Own Heart." David lived a very faithful life to the Lord from his early years as a shepherd boy, tending the sheep in the pastures. David stood against the great giant, Goliath, single-handedly with his slingshot and five river stones when the entire Israelite army was terrified to go against him. After his great victory over Goliath he was assigned by King Saul to lead his army. God's hand and favor were clearly upon David as He protected him numerous times from the jealous hand of King Saul. Eventually, King Saul was brought to his death and David was raised up to succeed him as king.

While King David led Israel in a mighty way, not even David was so great that he was not susceptible to temptation. When we begin to fall out of step with the Spirit we begin to approach a slippery slope. That is exactly what happened with King David. I have created a video lesson on the mistakes that David made and you can avoid. You can find it at www.damascusreport.com by going to the Bible Study tab and look for the lesson titled, "A Man After God's Own Heart...SINS!?" The steps that led David into sin is not what I want to discuss now, rather let us look at what happened afterward. David not only committed adultery with one of his top, most loyal soldier's wife, but he went so far as to have him murdered. This was a grievous act against the Lord. Sin separates us from the Father as we can see in scripture -Exodus 32:33, Micah 3:4; Isaiah 59:2; and 1 Corinthians 15:17.

Bless the Lord that He is a loving Father whose heart desires reconciliation. The Lord sent the prophet, Nathan, to rebuke David and warn him to repent. I encourage you to read about this entire story in 2 Samuel 11-14, and on. Nathan tells David a parable that represents him and the sins he carried out. After completing the parable Nathan asks David what should be done to the man who committed evil. David replied, "As the Lord lives, the man who has done this deserves to die and he shall restore the lamb fourfold, because he did this thing, and because he had not pity." 2 Samuel 12:5-6

Here is Nathan's reply to King David [7]"You are that man! Thus says the Lord, the God of Israel, 'I anointed you king over Israel, and I delivered you out of the hand of Saul. [8]And I gave you your master's house and your master's wives into your arms and gave you the house of Israel and of Judah. And if this were too little, I would add to you as much more. [9]Why have you despised the word of the Lord, to do what is evil in his sight? You have struck down Uriah the Hittite with the sword and have taken his wife to be your wife and have killed him with the sword of the Ammonites. ¹⁰Now therefore the sword shall never depart from your house, because you have despised me and have taken the wife of Uriah the Hittite to be your wife.' ¹¹Thus says the Lord, 'Behold, I will raise up evil against you out of your own house. And I will take your wives before your eyes and give them to your neighbor, and he shall lie with your wives in the sight of this sun. ¹²For you did it secretly, but I will do this thing before all Israel and before the sun.' ¹³David said to Nathan, "I have sinned against the Lord." And Nathan said to David, "The Lord also has put away your sin; you shall not die. ¹⁴Nevertheless, because by this deed you have utterly scorned the Lord, the child who is born to you shall die." (Emphasis added.)

What just happened? David committed two very serious sins against the Lord -adultery and murder. Not only that, but he drug another man, Joab, into his crime by commanding that he carry out the murder of Uriah by placing him at the front lines in a precarious situation knowing that it would result in death. Here is what I want you to see...even though David, the "man after God's own heart," committed very serious crimes against the Lord, as soon as he was aware of his iniquity he repented. He recognized that what he did was not only sin, but that it separated him from the Father. Do you see what happened here? David sinned. This brought separation between Him and the God whose heart he was after all his life. The Father loved David enough and knew his heart, that his heart was softened for God, even though he messed up. In knowing his heart, the Father sent the prophet, Nathan, to reveal to David that what he had done was wrong and that he needed to repent. David had a choice to either pridefully reject this warning or humble himself before the Lord and repent and receive His forgiveness. He did just that. Although David did suffer some serious consequences, he was ultimately restored to God. The heart of the Father.

Friend, I want you to hear me today. There is no sin that is greater than the blood of Jesus. There is no sin that is too big for what the blood has already covered. You only need to humble yourself, confess it, repent it, and be reconciled to the Father. Please, do not delay. If you know of sin that you have committed, humble yourself right now and speak to the Father. You can say something like this if you are unsure of what to say:

"Father, I love you so much. My heart's desire is to honor and glorify You and You alone. I confess that I...(insert sin). I repent of...(insert sin). I ask and humbly receive your forgiveness that Your Son's blood has already paid for. I will never pick this thing up again and will honor You with my life. Thank You Father for reconciling my heart to Yours. Amen."

Now, receive the Father's love and forgiveness. Walk no more in shame and condemnation as those are lies from Satan. Walk confidently in your sonship of Jesus Christ as one who has been washed clean, your past expunged. Be reconciled.

PRODIGAL RETURN

His father saw him and felt compassion." (Luke 15:20) "He was lost, and is found." (v. 24) What a glorious testimony of the Father's heart! I can so relate to the prodigal son. I willfully and somewhat knowingly chose a life outside of the Father's will. While I had not necessarily been taught how to walk in the way of the Lord or how to have relationship with Him, deep in my conscience I believe I knew that the way I was living was sinful. I did feel conviction for actions, just as the prodigal son did.

While this particular parable in Luke 15 does not exhibit outright judgment by the Father it does portray how natural consequences can often serve as discipline; which, eventually leads to reconciliation. Here is part of the parable form Luke 15.

[11]And he said, "There was a man who had two sons. [12]And the younger of them said to his father, 'Father, give me the share of property that is coming to me.' And he divided his property between them. [13]Not many days later, the younger son gathered all he had and took a journey into a far country, and there he squandered his property in reckless living. [14]And

when he had spent everything, a severe famine arose in that country, and he began to be in need. ¹⁵ So he went and hired himself out to one of the citizens of that country who sent him into his fields to feed pigs. ¹⁶ And he was longing to be fed with the pods that the pigs ate, and no one gave him anything."

¹⁷"But when he came to himself, he said, 'How many of my father's hired servants have more than enough bread, but I perish here with hunger! ¹⁸ I will arise and go to my father and I will say to him, "Father, I have sinned against heaven and before you. ¹⁹ I am no longer worthy to be called your son. Treat me as one of your hired servants." ²⁰ And he arose and came to his father. But while he was still a long way off, his father saw him and felt compassion, and ran and embraced him and kissed him. ²¹And the son said to him, 'Father, I have sinned against heaven and before you (emphasis added). I am no longer worthy to be called your son.' ²²But the father said to his servants, 'Bring quickly the best robe and put it on him, and put a ring on his hand, and shoes on his feet. ²³And bring the fattened calf and kill it, and let us eat and celebrate.'"
Skipping to v. ³²"It was fitting to celebrate and be glad for this your brother was dead, and is alive; he was lost, and is found."

The son was greedy and wanted his inheritance early so that he could go into the world and party and blow all of his money. I am sure that his father knew that it was not a good idea but the son's father could not make that decision for him. The son had to come to a place where he was humble enough in his own heart that he was ready to receive the love of the father. He recklessly spent all that he had and ultimately ended up in a dire situation, starving with no home. All of this could have been avoided if he had been humble and most likely heeded his father's instructions. But, like many of us, he thought he knew it all. So, he suffered very real and harsh consequences for his stubbornness and pride. But it was in the worst of that situation that his spirit was convicted of his arrogance and foolishness. In verses eighteen and nineteen when he is rehearsing what he will say to his father he had already come to a place of repentance in his heart. He goes to his father prepared to be hired as a servant and not treated like a son.

Before the son can even make it all the way to the house the father sees him and runs to him with arms wide open. He kisses him and receives him. The son confesses and repents to his father and to God. His father then responds with great celebration! Hallelujah! This is exactly how our heavenly Fatherly responds to us when we humble ourselves, repent and return to Him.

Let us break down what just happened.

- The son, in greed and arrogance, went out into the world and recklessly spent all he had, committed sins and went in the opposite direction of the father.
- The son suffered very real consequences for his actions, which broke down the walls of pride and greed.
- The son was convicted in his spirit and was led into repentance.
- The father, knowing his son's heart, ran to him and welcomed him with open arms and a kiss.
- Reconciliation happened.

What a beautiful testimony of the heart of the Father! This parable represents the heart of our heavenly Father. No matter how big we mess up, if we humble ourselves and come to a heart posture of repentance, and seek the Lord, He is quick to forgive, forget, and celebrate. Our Father desires reconciliation.

SAUL TO PAUL

Probably one of my most favorite transformations of all time is that of Saul of Tarsus. Here we have a very prominent, extremely educated, super influential, Jewish by birth and well renowned religious zealot of a man who was at the forefront of Christian persecution. He was terrorizing those who followed "The Way." Under his orders, many believers were killed. He absolutely did not recognize Jesus Christ of Nazareth to be the Son of God. In fact, he recognized him to be crazy. We have a man that you never would have expected would become a man totally sold-out for Jesus. How on earth did such a thing come to pass?

In Acts 9 we read the miraculous, supernatural encounter that Saul had, in front of his peers mind you, with Jesus, just shortly after he ravages a church. It would have seemed that there was no way that Saul would ever renounce his vengeful faith, yet...God. God busted into the scene knocking down every obstacle. There are times when cases call for extreme actions; this was definitely one of them. Unless Saul was wrecked spiritually by Jesus he probably never would have experienced a heart transformation. When he was knocked down by the powerful light on the way to Damascus his heart was also knocked down and the softening began. He heard the voice of Jesus, challenging him, "Saul, Saul, why are you persecuting me?" (Acts 9:4). He was temporarily blinded and needing help to move about. Jesus proceeded to give him instructions for what to do next. Now, Saul could very easily have rejected these instructions and moving in pride and a hard heart, he could have refused to submit. However, his heart being softened, he felt compelled to submit to the orders to go to the city and await further instruction.

Saul sat blinded, fasting, praying and seeing visions for three days, waiting...all while his heart continued to be softened. Ananias received instruction from the Lord to go to Straight Street and tend to Saul. Ananias had the choice to reject God's instructions or stop what he was doing and partner with the Lord in His work. He chose to partner with the Lord after some doubt considering whom he knew this man to be. The Lord says something intriguing in verses fifteen and sixteen, "But the Lord said to him, "Go, for he is a chosen instrument of mine to carry my name before the Gentiles and kings and the children of Israel. 16 For I will show him how much he must suffer for the sake of my name."

Although Saul was in the process of having open-heart surgery by the Great Physician it was made clear that there would be some real consequences for his previous actions. While we cannot understand all of it, or why God chooses to allow some to suffer and others not to, we must recognize that He is God and we are not. He has the right to do whatever He wants. But it was very clear that for all the persecution and evil that Saul carried out against God and His people, he would suffer for it. Many churches and pastors do not like to teach this aspect of scripture today. They want you to believe that you will never have to suffer for what you have done. That is just not scriptural.

Moving on to the more exciting part of the heart transformation!

Acts 9
^{17}So Ananias departed and entered the house. And laying his hands on him he said, "Brother Saul, the Lord Jesus who appeared to you on the road by which you came has sent me so that you may regain your sight and be filled with the Holy Spirit." ^{18}And immediately something like scales fell from his eyes, and he regained his sight. Then he rose and was baptized; ^{19}taking food, he was strengthened. (Emphasis added)

As the Lord softened Saul's heart each step of the way this word of knowledge spoken by Ananias confirmed for Saul that this was definitely an act of God which further softened his heart for the Lord. Obviously repentance took place in his heart, whether he verbally repented or not, the Father clearly knew that his heart was repentant. Saul not only became a follower of The Way, which he was persecuting just hours before, but he also became baptized with the Holy Spirit! After this amazing event Saul went on to proclaim Jesus in the Synagogues! Can you imagine? We see that in chapter thirteen, verse nine that Saul becomes known as Paul and is referred to as such from that point on.

Breaking this miraculous event down, let us see the heart of the Father.
- Saul persecutes The Way.
- The Lord visits Saul on the way to Damascus, blinding him, and instructing him, all while his heart is being worked on by the Physician.
- Visions and words of knowledge confirm for Saul that this is indeed the working of the Lord.
- Saul's heart is repentant and yielded to God.
- Saul regains his sight, physically and spiritually...he was reconciled to the Father and then begins to partner with the Father.

WOW! Have you done something so horrible that you believe that you are unforgivable? Have you done something so awful that you think there is no way that God can receive you as His son or daughter? Look at what Saul had done? He not only persecuted Christians, but he persecuted Jesus and His church! He ordered Christians to be executed! Yet, here we see that the Father's heart desires reconciliation. Saul humbled himself into repentance and submitted to the Lord. He then partnered with the Lord in His kingdom work.

What have you done that is separating you form the Father? What have you done that has painted your past as unforgivable? Hear me friend...NOTHING! There is nothing so awful that Jesus' blood can't cover it. (Well, there is one unpardonable sin...that is blaspheming the Holy Spirit. A whole different lesson for another day, but it can be found in the Word). Your sin is not bigger than God. If it was, then He would not be God. All you have to do is humble yourself, repent of your sin and submit to the Lord. He is ready to receive you with open arms. Just reach out to Him. Just talk to Him. Receive His love now.

FATHER KNOWS BEST

It is apparent by now that we, as humans, descendants of Adam and Eve, are born with a sin nature. But there is hope found in the only Son of God, the Father. At birth, we are condemned to hell because of our sin nature. We must be reconciled to the Father and accept the forgiveness of our sins by the blood that was shed by Jesus Christ, the Son of God. Our Father loves us so much. He wants none of us to perish. Imagine a Father who is willing to forgive the worst of sins and welcome you into His genealogy and inheritance. Wow!

Let me show you just how much the Father loves you:

John 3:16 For God so loved the world, that he gave his only Son, that whoever believes in him should not perish but have eternal life. [17] For God did not send his Son into the world to condemn the world, but in order that the world might be saved through him. [18] Whoever believes in him is not condemned, but whoever does not believe is condemned already, because he has not believed in the name of the only Son of God. [19] And this is the judgment: the light has come into the world, and people loved the darkness rather than the light because their works were evil. [20] For everyone who does wicked things hates the light and does not come to the light, lest his works should be exposed. [21] But whoever does what is true comes to the light, so that it may be clearly seen that his works have been carried out in God." (Emphasis added)

There are only two kingdoms in all of existence-The Kingdom of Light (God, righteousness) and the kingdom of darkness, (Satan, evil). We must choose which kingdom we will walk in. We must accept the free gift of mercy through the shed blood of Jesus Christ, which pardons our sins and expunges our record of unrighteousness. We must also set Jesus as Lord over every area of our lives. Just stopping at receiving His blood for the forgiveness of our sins is not walking into the fullness of the gift our Father has prepared for us.

Romans eight explains how we are to live our life in the Spirit, which is congruent to the Kingdom of Light.

[1]There is therefore now no condemnation for those who are in Christ Jesus. [2]For the law of the Spirit of life has set you free in Christ Jesus from the law of sin and death. [3]For God has done what the law, weakened by the flesh, could not do. By sending his own Son in the likeness of sinful flesh and for sin, he condemned sin in the flesh, [4]in

order that the righteous requirement of the law might be fulfilled in us, <u>who walk not according to the flesh but according to the Spirit.</u> ⁵For those <u>who live according to the flesh set their minds on the things of the flesh</u>, but those <u>who live according to the Spirit set their minds on the things of the Spirit</u>. ⁶For <u>to set the mind on the flesh is death</u>, but <u>to set the mind on the Spirit is life and peace</u>. ⁷For the mind that is set on the flesh is hostile to God, for it does not submit to God's law; indeed, it cannot. ⁸Those who are in the flesh cannot please God. ⁹You, however, are not in the flesh but in the Spirit, if in fact the Spirit of God dwells in you. <u>Anyone who does not have the Spirit of Christ does not belong to him.</u> ¹⁰But if Christ is in you, although the body is dead because of sin, the Spirit is life because of righteousness. ¹¹If the Spirit of him who raised Jesus from the dead dwells in you, he who raised Christ Jesus from the dead will also give life to your mortal bodies through his Spirit who dwells in you.

Heirs with Christ

¹²So then, brothers, we are debtors, not to the flesh, to live according to the flesh. ¹³For if you live according to the flesh you will die, but if by the Spirit you put to death the deeds of the body, you will live. ¹⁴<u>For all who are led by the Spirit of God are sons of God.</u> ¹⁵For you did not receive the spirit of slavery to fall back into fear, but you have received the Spirit of adoption as sons, by whom we cry, "Abba! Father!" ¹⁶The Spirit

himself bears witness with our spirit that we are children of God, [17]and if children, then heirs—heirs of God and fellow heirs with Christ, provided we suffer with him in order that we may also be glorified with him.

Future Glory

[18]For I consider that the sufferings of this present time are not worth comparing with the glory that is to be revealed to us [19]For, the creation waits with eager longing for the revealing of the sons of God. [20]For the creation was subjected to futility, not willingly, but because of him who subjected it, in hope [21]that the creation itself will be set free from its bondage to corruption and obtain the freedom of the glory of the children of God. [22]For we know that the whole creation has been groaning together in the pains of childbirth until now. [23]And not only the creation, but we ourselves, who have the firstfruits of the Spirit, groan inwardly as we wait eagerly for adoption as sons, the redemption of our bodies. [24]For in this hope we were saved. Now hope that is seen is not hope. For who hopes for what he sees? [25]But if we hope for what we do not see, we wait for it with patience. [26]Likewise the Spirit helps us in our weakness. For we do not know what to pray for as we ought, but the Spirit himself intercedes for us with groanings too deep for words. [27]And he who searches hearts knows what is the mind of the Spirit, because the Spirit intercedes for the saints according to the will of God. [28]And we

know that for those who love God all things work together for good, for those who are called according to his purpose. ²⁹For those whom he foreknew he also predestined to be conformed to the image of his Son, in order that he might be the firstborn among many brothers. ³⁰And those whom he predestined he also called, and those whom he called he also justified, and those whom he justified he also glorified.

God's Everlasting Love

³¹What then shall we say to these things? If God is for us, who can be against us? ³²He who did not spare his own Son but gave him up for us all, how will he not also with him graciously give us all things? ³³ Who shall bring any charge against God's elect? It is God who justifies. ³⁴Who is to condemn? Christ Jesus is the one who died—more than that, who was raised—who is at the right hand of God, who indeed is interceding for us. ³⁵Who shall separate us from the love of Christ? Shall tribulation, or distress, or persecution, or famine, or nakedness, or danger, or sword? ³⁶As it is written, "For your sake we are being killed all the day long; we are regarded as sheep to be slaughtered." ³⁷ No, in all these things we are more than conquerors through him who loved us. ³⁸For I am sure that neither death nor life, nor angels nor rulers, nor things present nor things to come, nor powers, ³⁹nor height nor depth, nor anything else in all creation, will be able to separate us from the love of God in Christ Jesus our Lord.

Here are more verses that tell of His great love!

Deuteronomy 7:9 Know, therefore that the Lord your God is God, the faithful God who keeps covenant and steadfast love with those who love him and keep his commandments, to a thousand generations,

Psalm 86:15 But you, O' Lord, are a God merciful and gracious, slow to anger and abounding in steadfast love and faithfulness.

John 3:16 "For God so loved the world, that he gave his only Son, that whoever believes in Him should not perish but have eternal life.

Romans 5:8 ...but God shows His love for us in that while we were still sinners, Christ died for us. ^{9}Since, therefore, we have now been justified by his blood, much more shall we be saved by Him from the wrath of God. ^{10}For if while we were enemies we were reconciled to God by the death of His Son, much more, now that we are reconciled, shall we be saved by his life. ^{11}More than that, we also rejoice in God through our Lord Jesus Christ, through whom we now received reconciliation. (One of my most favorite scriptures! Emphasis added)

Galatians 2:20 I have been crucified with Christ. It is no longer I who live, but Christ who lives in me. And the life I now live in the flesh I live by faith in the Son of God, who loved me and gave himself for me.

Ephesians 2:4 But God, being rich in mercy, because of the great love with which He loved us, 5even when we were dead in our trespasses, made us alive together with Christ - by grace you have been saved—6and raised up with Him and seated us with Him in the heavenly places in Christ Jesus, 7so that in the coming ages He might show the immeasurable riches of his grace in kindness toward us in Christ Jesus. 8For by grace you have been saved through faith. And this is not your own doing; it is the gift of God, 9not a result of works, so that no one may boast 10For we are His workmanship, created in Christ Jesus for good works, which God prepared beforehand, that we should walk in them.

1 John 3:1 See what kind of love the Father has given to us, that we should be called children of God; and so we are. The reason why the world does not know us is that it did not know Him.

Do you see the expression in His love for us? Do you realize that He will go to great lengths to express and establish His love for you? Our Father will do whatever it takes to knock down every obstacle that is keeping us separated from Him. That is a Father who is faithful and determined. When we begin to realize just how much He loves, that He actually gave His one and only Son to die in our place, to pay for our sins...then we can begin to walk in the reality of not only who He is but, who we are in Him! This is huge! We do not have to be condemned to hell. We do not have to accept a punishment that He redeemed us from. If we will ignore the lies of the enemy and accept His truth we cannot only begin to walk in His love, but we can also walk in His freedom and liberty. We can live a life in the Spirit that allows us to be liberated from sin and condemnation. Hallelujah!

As we begin to understand and fathom the love that our Father has for us we begin to learn how to love ourselves which in turn, allows us to love others instead of always being offended or hurt by them. When we realize His love for us and that it frees us from condemnation and shame, we begin to love freely, without expectation. We can say to someone, "I love you," and not need to hear it back! What a release! We realize and accept that we have been washed in the blood of Jesus and our past has been wiped completely away. We realize we are no longer a lowly, condemned, wretched sinner; rather we are children of God, co-heirs with Christ Jesus, seated in heavenly places at the right hand of the Father! That is something to celebrate my friend!

Once we begin to walk in this new identity in Christ we realize that those who have yet to accept His free gift are still in bondage and walking with the kingdom of darkness. When this reality sets in we can then understand that those people cannot be expected to act like someone who is saved. We recognize that they know not what they do and that we cannot respond to them in the flesh, but rather in the Spirit, with the mind and heart of Christ with reconciliation being the goal. Wow! So, when someone does something that might be offensive or hurtful we no longer take offense to it or get hurt by it...we recognize that they are hurting and in desperate need of the Father's love and salvation. Instead of fighting back or seeking vengeance we choose to love them right where they are, just as God loved us while we were yet still sinners. We show them the love of God in how we live and respond to them. Our prayer and hope is that they see Christ in us, the hope of glory and desire the same for themselves.

Why all this talk of reconciliation if Jesus paid for everyone to be free? Here is the thing to consider - just because Jesus paid everyone's ransom does not mean that everyone has accepted His free gift. It is not enough to just accept the free gift of salvation as a means of fire insurance, and continue to live in bondage and sin. God has created a way for us to have life and life more abundantly, here on earth and in heaven. There must be a genuine heart transformation. Reconciliation is needed because at birth we are all separated from God by our sin nature. Unless we accept His blood sacrifice and accept Jesus as our Lord and Savior we will continue to be separated from Him and condemned to hell for all eternity. We must be reconciled to the Father through His Son, Jesus Christ. We must set Him as Lord over every single area of our life and walk with him and partner with Him in His Kingdom of Light. The truth of the matter is, not everyone will be going to heaven and spending eternity with God.

There are only two kingdoms in all of creation, the kingdom of darkness, which is under the authority of Satan, yet submitted to God; and the Kingdom of Light, which is under the authority of God. However, both kingdoms are submitted to God. Satan has absolutely no authority over God, His Kingdom, Jesus, or disciples of Jesus Christ. Colossians 1:13-14 tells us, "He has delivered us from the domain of darkness and transferred us to the kingdom of His beloved Son, [14]in whom we have redemption, the forgiveness of sins." We either partner with darkness or with light. It is impossible to walk in two opposite directions, period. In order to walk with the Kingdom of God we must first be reconciled to Him through the blood of His Son, Jesus Christ. Please, if you have not been reconciled to the Father, do not delay. Please stop reading right now and talk with the Father.

FORGIVENESS, NOT AN OPTION

This discussion on reconciliation cannot be had without also discussing forgiveness. Reconciliation is impossible without forgiveness. The whole point of the cross was reconciliation which, included forgiveness. Our Father wiped away all of our sins with the blood of His Son, Jesus Christ. Once we were redeemed by His blood we were reconciled to the Father. God cannot be in relationship with someone who is stained by sin or walking willfully in habitual sin. The only way to be in relationship with God is to be washed clean of sin. This can only happen with the blood of His Son. As we saw in earlier scriptures already mentioned we were wretched in our own sins, dirty, filthy; yet, our Father forgave us while we were in the midst of our wretched state. God commands us to do the very same thing with one another. Our sins are no lighter or less damning than our neighbor's. Our neighbor's sin is not beyond redemption just as ours are not. One thing we must understand is that forgiveness is not an option. We are commanded to forgive, even to forgive our enemies. Let us see what God's Word says about forgiveness.

Matthew 6:14-15 For, if you forgive other people when they sin against you, your heavenly Father will also forgive you. 15 But if you do not forgive others their sins, your Father will not forgive your sins. (Emphasis added). Wow! That is heavy! It is also very clear...forgiveness is not an option.

Luke 17:3-4 So watch yourselves. "If your brother or sister sins against you, rebuke them; and if they repent, forgive them. 4 Even if they sin against you seven times in a day and seven times come back to you saying 'I repent,' you MUST forgive them." (Emphasis added)

Ephesians 4:31-32 Get rid of all bitterness, rage and anger, brawling and slander, along with every form of malice. 32 Be kind and compassionate to one another, forgiving each other, just as in Christ God forgave you. (Emphasis added)

Mark 11:25 "And when you stand praying, if you hold anything against anyone, <u>forgive</u> them, so that <u>your Father in heaven may forgive you</u> your sins." (Emphasis added). Notice this does not say only forgive them if they repent to you. It simply says, "If you hold anything against anyone....forgive." If you have held offense to someone for something they said or did...forgive them, period. (Emphasis added)

Colossians 3:13 Bear with each other and forgive one another if any of you has a grievance against someone. Forgive as the Lord forgave you. (Emphasis added)

Again, nowhere does this last verse say that we are to wait for the offender to repent or apologize. It simply tells us to forgive them. In fact, this tells us that if WE have a grievance against someone...the responsibility falls on us and we need to forgive them without the offender ever coming to us and apologizing or repenting. Is this not what God did for us?

How is this fair you say? Fair? Do you believe that the gift of eternal salvation that you will receive at the end of this earthly life is fair considering the sins you have committed against God, the creator of all things? That is, if you have received His free gift of salvation and have set Him as Lord over every area of your life. Whether it seems fair or not, we are commanded to forgive others. Whether they have apologized or repented, we are commanded to forgive others. Whether they are even aware of the offense they committed against us, we are commanded to forgive others. Why is this so important? The very nature of God, the very thing He did for us, He is calling us to do for others...forgive. There is healing in forgiveness. In fact, we cannot be forgiven if we do not forgive others. Please, do not miss this. Forgiveness is not an option.

You may be struggling with this concept, this command, to forgive others who have not even acknowledged that they need it. What does God's Word tell us about how we should treat others; including those who have offended us or committed a sin against us, or our loved ones? You may recognize the following scripture from a previous chapter...

2 Corinthians 5:14-21 For the love of Christ controls us, because we have concluded this: that one has died for all, therefore all have died; [15] and He died for all, that those who live might no longer live for themselves <u>but for Him</u> who for their sake died and was raised. (Is the love of Christ truly controlling us? Emphasis added)

16 From now on, therefore, we regard no one according to the flesh. Even though we once regarded Christ according to the flesh, we regard Him thus no longer. [17]Therefore, if anyone is in Christ, he is a new creation. The old has passed away; behold, the new has come. [18]All this is from God, who through Christ reconciled us to Himself and <u>gave us the ministry of reconciliation</u>; [19]that is in Christ God was reconciling the world to Himself, not counting their trespasses against them, and entrusting to us the message of reconciliation. [20] Therefore, we are ambassadors for Christ, God making His appeal through us. We implore you on behalf of

Christ, be reconciled to God. ²¹For our sake He made Him to be sin who knew no sin, so that in Him we might become the righteousness of God. (Emphasis added)

Romans 8:5-17 For those who live according to the flesh set their minds on the things of the flesh, but those who live according to the Spirit set their minds on the things of the Spirit. ⁶For to set their mind on the flesh is death, but to set the mind on the Spirit is life and peace. ⁷ For <u>the mind that is set on the flesh is hostile to God</u>, for it does not submit to God's law; <u>indeed, it cannot</u>. ⁸<u>Those who are in the flesh cannot please God</u>.

⁹ You, however, <u>are not in the flesh but in the Spirit, if in fact the Spirit of God dwells in you</u>. Anyone who does not have the Spirit of Christ does not belong to Him. 10 But if Christ is in you, although the body is dead because of sin, the Spirit is life because of righteousness. ¹¹ If the Spirit of Him who raised Jesus from the dead dwells in you, He who raised Christ Jesus from the dead will also give life to your mortal bodies through His Spirit who dwells in you. (The same Spirit that rose Christ from the dead lives in YOU!)

¹² So then, brothers, we are debtors, not to the flesh, to live according to the flesh. ¹³ For if you live according to the flesh you will die, but if by the Spirit you put to death the deeds of the body, you will live. ¹⁴ For all who are led by the

Spirit of God are sons of God. 15 For you did not receive the spirit of slavery to fall back into fear, but you have received the Spirit of adoption as sons, by whom we cry, "Abba! Father!." 16 The Spirit Himself bears witness with our spirit that we are children of God, 17 and if children, then heirs - hears of God and fellow heirs with Christ, provided we suffer with Him in order that we may also be glorified with him. (Hallelujah! Emphasis added)

So, if we are truly saved by His grace, by His blood, and we truly have the Spirit of Christ living in us then we should be walking by the Spirit and not by the flesh. This means that we also no longer regard others according to the flesh, rather by the Spirit. And those who are not saved, we do not expect to act as though they were saved. We choose to show mercy and grace just as He showed us and continues to shows us. Let us be real...we have each failed at some point in our Christian walk. We have moments just as the apostles did; some of us are more like Peter, and have many moments. Keeping this in mind, we must stop treating others, especially our brothers and sisters, as though they are held to a higher standard. In fact, they fall under the same saving blood as we do even though none of us really "deserve" it. So, forgive...it is not an option, rather a command.

RECONCILIATION IN RELATIONSHIPS

The heart of reconciliation is not just for man and God. The heart of the Father clearly shows us that He desires that we be reconciled to one another as well. If we are to be the body of Christ, the Church, we must be united in one Spirit, as scripture tells us. Ephesians 4:4 says, "There is one body and one Spirit - just as you were called to the one hope that belongs to your call-" Also in Psalm 133 we see how important unity is to the Father - "Behold, how good and pleasant it is when brothers dwell in unity! ²It is like precious oil on the head, running down on the beard, on the beard of Aaron, running down on the collar of robes! ³It is like the dew of Hermon, which falls on the mountains of Zion! For there the Lord has commanded the blessing, life forevermore." Wow! Unity among the brethren receives the command of blessing and life forevermore from the Lord! That is something to be celebrated. How do we attain unity?

Unity cannot happen unless reconciliation happens where there is dissension. First, reconciliation must happen for the individual to the Father and secondly, reconciliation for the body of believers, among individuals. There is nothing more divisive and more corrosive than disunity among the brethren. Mark tells us in chapter three, verse five, "And if a house is divided against itself, that house will not be able to stand." Have you ever been to a church where you could feel the disunity in the air? Not pleasant right? I have been to churches that suffered from this very thing and those churches are no longer in operation today or are very close to completely falling apart. The presence of the Lord was nowhere to be found in those churches. The same is true for families; which is why we see devastating divorce rates today. We must learn to seek and experience reconciliation within our personal relationships after we are reconciled individually to the Father.

I get it, it is not always easy to attain reconciliation, especially when it involves another person. We cannot control how others will act or react. We can only be responsible for our actions and responses to others. In Romans chapter twelve, verse eighteen we are instructed, "If possible, so far as it depends on YOU, live peaceably with all." (Emphasis added). Whew! We are called to be the peacemakers. We are instructed to do everything within our own power to live at peace with ALL. That means everyone. That means that person that absolutely rubs your skin raw every time you are near them. That means your family, your neighbor, your church, and even your enemy.

If you have committed an offense against someone you need to go to them and confess your sin and ask their forgiveness. If they refuse to forgive you, that is on them and our Father will deal with them. It is not our place to hold judgment over them or to try and force them to respond with forgiveness. We must remember that there is only one Judge and we are not Him. If you have done your part and made every effort to confess, apologize, and make amends, then you walk away peacefully and let Holy Spirit do His work while you wait patiently. We must protect ourselves from becoming consumed with this person's response or lack thereof. This can provide an entry for the spirit of bitterness to take up root in our heart which breeds hardness and separation between us and the Father. We must trust that Holy Spirit knows best how to handle the other person's heart. Occasionally it may be necessary or effective to bring in a pastor or church leadership or a trusted mutual friend who can facilitate a conversation between the two of you in private. If that is not effective then move on as you trust Holy Spirit to work in the situation.

We are called to love with Jesus love, unconditional love that is full of grace and mercy. We are to allow God to be judge as we submit to His authority and Word. Again, in Romans chapter twelve, verses fourteen through twenty-one let us learn: "Bless those who persecute you; bless and do not curse them. 15 Rejoice with those who rejoice, weep with those who weep. 16Live in harmony with one another. Do not be haughty, but associate with the lowly. Never be wise in your own sight. 17Repay no one evil for evil, but give thought to do what is honorable in the sight of all. 18If possible, so far as it depends on you, live peaceably with all. 19Beloved, never avenge yourselves, but leave it the wrath of God, for it is written, 'Vengeance is mine, I will repay, says the Lord,' 20 To the contrary, 'if your enemy is hungry, feed him; if he is thirsty, give him something to drink; for by so doing you will heap burning coals on his head.' 21Do not be overcome by evil, but overcome evil with good."

We are called to be peacemakers and if we accept that call we will be called sons of God (Matthew 5:9). Listen to the words of our Messiah, Jesus..." 21'You have heard that it was said to those of old, "You shall not murder; and whoever murders will be liable to judgment." 22But I say to you that everyone who is angry with his brother will be liable to judgment; whoever insults his brother will be liable to the council; and whoever says, "You fool!" Will be liable to the hell of fire. 23So if you are offering your gift at the altar and there remember that your brother has something against you, 24leave your gift there before the altar and go. First be reconciled to your brother, and then come and offer your gift." (Emphasis added). Our goal is to share the heart of the Father, which is always reconciliation.

Colossians 1:19-22 "For in Him all the fullness of God was pleased to dwell, [20] and through Him to reconcile to Himself all things, whether on earth or in heaven, making peace by the blood of His cross. [21]And you, who once were alienated and hostile in mind, doing evil deeds, [22]He has now reconciled in His body of flesh by His death, in order to present you holy and blameless and above reproach before Him." (Emphasis added).

Do you see how important reconciliation is to the Father? Do you see how reconciliation is the message of the cross? Jesus gave His life, His blood, in order that we might be reconciled to the Father through His perfect sacrifice. The Father is calling us to do the same thing with one another. Look at this profound and heart-piercing scripture from Second Corinthians.

2 Corinthians 5:16-21 "From now on, therefore, we regard no one according to the flesh. Even though we once regarded Christ according to the flesh, we regard Him thus no longer. [17] Therefore, if anyone is in Christ, he is a new creation. The old has passed away; behold, the new has come. [18]All this is from God, who through Christ reconciled us to Himself and gave US the ministry of reconciliation; [19] that is, in

Christ God was reconciling the world to Himself, <u>not counting their trespasses against them</u>, and entrusting to US the message of reconciliation. [20]Therefore, we are ambassadors for Christ, God making his appeal through us. We implore you on behalf of Christ, be reconciled to God. [21]For our sake He made him to be sin who knew no sin, so that in Him we might become the righteousness of God." (Emphasis added)

Talk about a loaded verse right? Let us break this down. Christ died on the cross in order that we might (we have to choose and accept this) be reconciled to the Father. He counts our trespasses no more. He then gave US, you and me, the ministry of reconciliation. What does that even mean? That means that not only are we to have a heart for others to be reconciled to the Father, but we are to have a heart to be reconciled with one another, living in peace and unity, not counting one another's trespasses. We are to carry the message of reconciliation to others. How on earth can we possibly carry the message of reconciliation if we are holding others' trespasses over them, not forgiving them? How can we carry the message of reconciliation if we are hating our brothers and sisters, our neighbors, or our family? What are we called to do?

Colossians 3:12-17 "Put on then, as God's chosen ones, holy and beloved, compassionate hearts, kindness, humility, meekness, and patience, ¹³ bearing with one another and, if one has a complaint against another, forgiving each other; <u>as the Lord has forgiven you, so you also must forgive</u>. ¹⁴And <u>above all these put on love</u>, which binds everything together in perfect harmony. ¹⁵And let the peace of Christ rule in your hearts, to which indeed you were called in one body. And be thankful. ¹⁶Let the word of Christ dwell in you richly, teaching and admonishing one another in all wisdom, singing psalms and hymns and spiritual songs, with thankfulness in your hearts to God. ¹⁷And whatever you do, in word or deed, do everything in the name of the Lord Jesus, giving thanks to God the Father through Him." (Emphasis added)

Hebrews 12:14-15 "Strive for peace with everyone, and for the holiness without which no one will see the Lord. ¹⁵See to it that no one fails to obtain the grace of God; that no "root of bitterness" springs up and causes trouble, and by it many become defiled...". (Emphasis added)

Luke 17:3-4 "Pay attention to yourselves! If your brother sins, rebuke him, and if he repents, forgive him, 4 and if he sins against you seven times in the day, and turns to you seven times, saying, 'I repent,' you must forgive him." (Emphasis added)

As we continue to be purified by the blood of Christ and sanctified (set apart as holy, made legitimate, purified) by the Holy Spirit we continue to mature spiritually. We begin to recognize and acknowledge that we were sinners, defiled and wretched, yet...Christ gave His life in order to wash away our past and expunge our record of sins. If He was willing to give His life for us to be freed, then we can surely find it in our hearts to forgive our brothers and sisters and even those who are not Christians, as we are called to live at peace with all.

Ephesians 2:11-22 "Therefore remember that at one time you Gentiles in the flesh, called 'the uncircumcision' by what is called the circumcision, which is made in the flesh by hands -^{12}remember that you were at that time separated from Christ, alienated from the commonwealth of Israel and strangers to the covenants of promise, having no hope and without God in the world. ^{13}But now in Christ Jesus you who once were far off have been brought near by the blood of Christ. ^{14}For He Himself is our peace, who has made us both one and has broken down in His flesh the dividing wall of hostility. ^{15}by abolishing the law of commandments expressed in ordinances, that He might create in Himself one new man in place of the two, so making peace, ^{16}and might reconcile us both to God in one body through the cross, thereby killing the hostility. ^{17}And he came and preached peace to you who were far off and peace to you those who were near. ^{18}For through him we both have access in one Spirit to the Father. ^{19}So then you are no longer strangers and aliens, but you are fellow citizens with the saints and members of the household of God. [20] built on the foundation of the apostles and prophets, Christ Jesus Himself being the cornerstone, [21]in whole the whole structure being joined together, rows into a holy temple in the Lord. [22]In Him you also are being built together into a dwelling place for God by the Spirit."

Clearly the heart of the Father is reconciliation. If you still have doubts...

Ezekiel 18:23 "Have I any pleasure in the death of the wicked, declares the Lord God, and not rather that he should turn from his way and live?

Ezekiel 33:11 "Say to them, As I live, declares the Lord God, I have no pleasure in the death of the wicked, but that the wicked turn from his way and live; turn back, turn back from your evil ways, for why will you die, O house of Israel?"

If the heart of the Father is that we each be reconciled to Him and then we each be reconciled to one another we ought to consider this command and set our hearts to do it. Through receiving this message from the Lord while preparing a lesson for church He completely wrecked my heart for the message of reconciliation. He revealed to me in my own personal life relationships that needed to be reconciled. I obeyed and attempted to confess and repent of my errors in each relationship that was revealed to me. Some of the relationships have been reconciled and some of them have yet to be. This is where I wait patiently and faithfully on Holy Spirit to do His work in their hearts, for I have done my part. I have released these people of holding any kind of burden over me any more. I have released the spirit of bitterness that was taking root in my heart. In the relationships where I was wronged, I have chosen to forgive and remember it no more. I have personally experienced peace because of this. Miraculously, while confessing my sins to a couple of people a nagging neurological pain that I had been experiencing in my neck and shoulders completely disappeared. The healing came AS I confessed and sought forgiveness, not as the person forgave me. Praise God!

I had no idea that pain was being caused by the weight of the bitterness and guilt I was carrying for so long. I am so thankful that Holy Spirit reveals such things to us so that we can carry out the ministry of reconciliation. Reconciliation is important for all parties involved not just for ourselves. Bitterness will begin by taking root in our heart and then permeating into our bones. It is heavy. It hinders. It destroys. It must be eradicated immediately.

I pray that as you allow the scriptures to soak into your heart that you allow Holy Spirit to reveal areas of reconciliation that need to be dealt with in your life. I pray that healing can take place and that relationships are restored. Remember, He gave US the ministry of reconciliation. That means not only are we to be reconciled with the Father, but we are to seek reconciliation with others. We are also to help others in being reconciled to people in their lives. As we step out in faith in this ministry of reconciliation I believe that our lives, our families, our communities, our churches and even our nations can be changed.

RECONCILIATION AS A NATION

We have learned how the heart of the Father is for all to be reconciled to Him. This is true for the individual as well as for the nations. We see throughout scripture how nations are affected when they reject the will of God or choose to walk in His will. When nations walk with the Kingdom of God they generally receive blessings. On the contrary, when they choose to go against God's will, a nation might experience His judgment, or at least, consequences for their wickedness.

Jeremiah 18:1-17 The word that came to Jeremiah from the Lord: 2 "Arise, and go down to the potter's house, and there I will let you hear my words." 3So I went down to the potter's house, and there he was working at his wheel. 4And the vessel he was making of clay was spoiled in the potter's hand, and he reworked it into another vessel, as it seemed good to the potter to do. 5Then the word of the Lord came to me: 6"O house of Israel, can I not do with you as the potter has done? (A Desire to reconcile the lost to Himself). Declares the Lord. Behold, like the clay in the potter's hand, so are you in my hand, O house of Israel. ⁷If at any time I declare concerning a nation or a kingdom, that I will pluck up and break down and destroy it, ⁸and if that nation, concerning which I have spoken, turns from its evil, I will relent (the process of reconciliation) of the disaster that I intended to do to it. ⁹And if at any time declare concerning a nation or a kingdom that I will build and plant it, ¹⁰and if it does evil in my sight, not listening to my voice, then I will relent of the good that I had intended to do it. (The process of rejecting the Lord and turning from His Kingdom, breaking reconciliation.) ¹¹Now, therefore, say to the men of Judah and the inhabitants of Jerusalem: 'Thus says the Lord, Behold, I am shaping disaster against you and devising a plan against you. Return, every one form his evil way, and amend your ways and your deed.' (Seeking reconciliation with the Lord through repentance and receiving forgiveness.) ¹²"But they say, 'That is in vain! We will follow our own plans, and will every one act according to the stubbornness of his evil heart.' ¹³"Therefore thus says the Lord:

Ask among the nations,
Who has heard the like of this?
The virgin Israel
has done a very horrible thing.
¹⁴Does the snow of Lebanon leave
the crags of Sirion?
Do the mountain waters run dry,
the cold flowing streams?
¹⁵But my people have forgotten me;

they make offerings to false
gods; they made them stumble in their ways,
in the ancient roads,
not the highway,
¹⁶making their land a horror,
a thing to be hissed at forever.
Everyone who passes by it is horrified
and shake his head.
¹⁷Like the east wind I will scatter
them
before the enemy.
I will show them my back, not my
face,
in the day of their calamity."
(Emphasis added)
Also, in Deuteronomy 11:13-17

¹³"And if you will indeed obey my commandments that I command you today, to love the Lord your God, and to serve him with all your heart and with all your soul, ¹⁴He will give the rain for your land in its season, the early rain and the later rain, that you may gather in your grain and your wine and your oil. ¹⁵ And he will give grass in your fields for your livestock, and you shall eat and be full. ¹⁶Take care lest your heart be deceived, and you turn aside and serve other gods and worship them; ¹⁷then the anger of the Lord will be kindled against you, and He will shut up the heavens, so that there will be no rain, and the land will yield no fruit, and you will perish quickly off the good land that the Lord is giving you. (Emphasis added)

You may be wondering what Deuteronomy eleven has to do with reconciliation. If we look at the meaning of reconciliation this may clear things up. The word, "reconcile," according to www.Meriam-Webster.com, means: to restore to friendship or harmony; to settle or to resolve; to make consistent or congruous; to account for. As we see in Deuteronomy eleven, a nation can be reconciled to the Lord by being restored to His friendship, by being in right standing with Him, or in harmony with Him and His ways. The only way this can be done is to be submitted to His Lordship, to His authority. This means that as a nation, or even as an individual, we can no longer walk with the kingdom of darkness, rather, we choose to walk with the Kingdom of God. We turn from our evil ways. We lay down our wicked habits and sin. We leave them at the cross and submit to the Holy Father. We begin to walk according to His commandments and laws.

2 Chronicles 7:11-22 Thus Solomon finished the house of the Lord and the king's house. All that Solomon had planned to do in the house of the Lord and in his own house he successfully accomplished. 12 Then the Lord appears to Solomon in the night and said to him: "I have heard your prayer and have chosen this place for myself as a house of sacrifice. 13 When I shut up the heavens so that there is no rain, or command the locust to devour the land, or send pestilence among my people, 14 <u>if my people who are called by my name humble themselves, and pray and</u>

seek my face and turn from their wicked ways, then I will hear form heaven and will forgive their sin and heal their land. ¹⁵ Now my eyes will be open and my ears attentive to the prayer that is made in this place. ¹⁶. For now I have chosen and consecrated this house that my name may be there forever. My eyes and my heart will be there for all time. ¹⁷ And as for you, if you will walk before me as David your father walked, doing according to all that I have commanded you and keeping my statutes and my rules, ¹⁸ then I will establish your royal throne, as I covenanted with David your father, saying, 'You shall not lack a man to rule Israel.'"

¹⁹ "But if you turn aside and forsake my statutes and my commands that I have set before you, and go and serve other gods and worship them, ²⁰ then I will pluck you up form my land that I have given you, and this house that I have consecrated for my name, I will cast out of my sight, and I will make it a proverb and a byword among all peoples. ²¹ And at this house, which was exalted, everyone passing by will be astonished and say 'Why has the Lord done thus to this land and to this house?'

²² Then they will say, 'Because they abandoned the Lord, the God of their fathers who brought them out of the land of Egypt, and laid hold on other gods and worshiped them and served them. Therefore he has brought all this disaster on them.'" (Emphasis added)

This particular scripture is one of my absolute favorites. It is the perfect instruction of what a person or a nation must do to be reconciled to the Lord. Once the nation humbles themselves, prays, turns from their wicked ways, and seeks the Lord's face THEN the Lord will hear them from heaven, forgive their sin, and heal their land. The way for a nation to be healed is to be reconciled to the Father. This is also true of the individual. A person can receive healing through the process of reconciliation. This may be physical healing, emotional, relational, or spiritual.

A nation whose leaders are blatantly rejecting God and His laws are bringing judgment upon the entire nation. But a nation whose leaders humble themselves, pray, seek God, and turn from their wicked ways, will be reconciled to God. What role does the average citizen have to play in this? As individuals and as church bodies we must intercede for our leaders and our nation as a whole.

1 Timothy 2:1-4 First of all, then, I urge that <u>supplications, prayers, intercessions, and thanksgivings</u> be made for all people, 2 for kings (presidents, prime ministers) and all who are in high positions (governors, senators, political leaders), that we may lead a peaceful and quiet life, godly and dignified in every way. 3 This is good, and it is pleasing in the sight of God our

Savior, 4 <u>who desires all people to be saved and to come to the knowledge of the truth.</u> (Emphasis added).

Our first order of business is to make supplications, intercessions, prayers and thanksgivings for all of our leaders. This includes the leaders that we disagree with or who we think are not doing a very good job...especially these leaders. We can do this individually and collectively with our church, our family and our neighbors. We can also offer prayer to our leaders through written letters or emails. Some leaders are open and receptive to receiving prayer in person in their office. You may consider organizing a monthly prayer meeting in your church to pray for our leaders. It is also a good idea to be aware of current political and global situations so that we can be praying effectively.

Another area that, we as disciples of Jesus Christ, can actively participate in is voting and communicating with our elected officials regarding bills that are being considered or working to reverse legislation that goes against God's will. Encourage your family, friends, church and neighbors to vote and be politically active. Teach your children about the political processes and how they too, can get involved. Finally, study candidates and their voting records and where they stand on crucial issues. If they have a record of voting against God's will or if they blatantly speak out against God's will, then do not support them. If they follow God's will, support them and promote them to people you know.

A nation who willingly goes against God can expect at some point to receive judgment for their actions. But, as we see in 2 Chronicles 7:14-15, a nation who will humble themselves, pray, seek God's face and turn from their wicked ways will be forgiven and receive healing in their land. Do not get discouraged by the actions of our leaders. Instead, turn your energy and efforts into "First of all" praying for our leaders and praying that as a nation we might be reconciled to God.

Psalm 33:12 Blessed is the nation whose God is the Lord...

WHAT NOW?

If you have read this far you may be wondering if you have actually been reconciled to the Lord. Or, perhaps you may have personal relationships that need to be reconciled. If you are not sure where to begin I would like to give you some encouragement. It is not difficult to attain reconciliation. There is no one particular method that must be followed, other than the blood of Jesus.

Begin by asking yourself if you are truly submitted to the Lord. This means every area of your life. Just because you may go to church, perhaps you have even been in church your whole life, that does not necessarily mean you are in relationship with Jesus. You may have even read the entire bible from cover to cover and can recite Scripture. This too, does not mean that you are in relationship with the Lord. Scripture shows us that it is impossible for God to be in relationship with someone who is stained by sin. Sin separates us from the Father. The only way to have our sin wiped away is to accept what Jesus Christ did on the cross at Calvary.

We believe that what God has shown us in His word about Jesus shedding His blood for our sins is real. We believe that Christ gave His life for us. We then accept this free gift of salvation with the full understanding that there is absolutely nothing we can do to earn it. Once we have believed this truth and accepted the free gift, we submit our lives to the Father, to the Lordship of Jesus Christ. We lay down every sin, every stronghold, every struggle. We repent of each one. Repenting means that we confess it and agree that Jesus' blood washes it away permanently, that means we never pick that sin up again, ever. If for whatever reason, we slip, we immediately recognize that error and follow the steps o repentance again.

As we become washed by the blood of Jesus we begin to be reconciled to the Father. We come into right standing with our Holy God. We begin to allow Holy Spirit to guide our thoughts, our hearts, our spirits, our actions...everything. As we begin to live by the Spirit, as we learned about in Romans 8, we begin to show this same grace and mercy that we received form the Father to others.

If you are unsure whether you have confessed everything ask Holy Spirit to reveal to you if there is any unconfessed sin in your life that needs to be repented of. Holy Spirit has a special way of communicating with our heart and showing us things. Listen for His response. It may come with an unction in your gut, or a memory. It may come through something someone says to you. Sometimes Holy Spirit will reveal things to us through dreams or visions. Just be attentive to what is happening all around you.

The very most important reconciliation is between us and the Father. Once we are reconciled to Him, we then ask Holy Spirit to show us areas in our personal life that need to be tended to. We may already be aware of relationships that are broken. It is the heart of the Father that all relationships be reconciled and healed. He desires unity and peace, especially among the brethren. So, begin by entering into a moment of prayer. Talk to the Father just as you talk to anyone else. Thank Him for the blood of Jesus that reconciled you to Him. Then, begin to ask Holy Spirit to reveal any broken relationships in your life. Ask Him to show you if you have hurt someone or offended someone in any way, or if anyone has hurt you that you are holding judgment over. After you ask this, just sit quietly for a moment and wait on Him. It may be that your answer comes later on.

Once it is revealed to you where a relationship is in need of reconciliation pray about how to approach the person after you repent to the Father of any wrongdoing you may have done. Pray for their heart to be softened and prepared for reconciliation. You may want to approach them in person, which is usually best. However, there are times this is not possible or times that this may actually cause even more pain. Be sensitive to this. Writing a letter may be more appropriate, or perhaps a phone call. Just remember that tone often gets lost or assumed in written communication. Sometime the person we have offended will refuse to talk to us. It may be that the person has passed away and there is no way for communication (Remember, communicating with the dead is divination which is demonic). That is alright, take this up with the Lord and confess your wrongdoing and receive forgiveness for it. Do not walk in shame or guilt for this offense anymore. Refuse to hear the little whispers of the devil that try to condemn you over and over for something the blood has already covered. He may even speak through the person or others, do not listen to or believe the lies that you are not forgiven or that you are forever condemned because of this error. That is simply not true.

What do you do if the person refuses to talk with your or refuse to forgive you? Pray for them. That is all. I do not recommend forcing conversation or forcing the issue. This will often times make things much worse. At this point you leave the rest of the work to Holy Spirit. He is really good at what He does. But, I want to strongly caution you to not allow bitterness to take up root in your heart if they refuse to respond or forgive. If you have done your part, then let it go and move on. I have found that praying blessings over that person moves my heart to a posture of love and grace and leaves no room for bitterness. In the beginning you may have to force yourself to pray for them. But over time, I promise you, it gets much easier.

In the following chapter I will provide you with some tools that may help you walk through reconciliation, forgiveness, and healing.

TOOLS
Open Chair Forgiveness

The following tool for forgiveness was exposed to me by my mentor, Jennifer Smallwood. The following are her words:

(This tool was not developed by me, but has been adapted from how I was shown. I have not been able to discover its origins.)

For if you forgive others for their transgressions, your heavenly Father will also forgive you. But if you do not forgive others, then your Father will not forgive your transgressions. Matthew 6:14-15

Forgiveness is not about the offender or the abuser but rather about which kingdom of law a believer chooses to live under. Romans 8:1-8 describes there is the law of sin and death and the law of life in Christ Jesus. The law of sin and death offered for there to be many judges with the primary accuser being the enemy. Forgiveness under the law of sin and death was demonstrated to be unachievable without Christ. The law of life in Christ Jesus requires that there only be one judge, the One who was without sin, and offers forgiveness only through his blood. Many seek to receive forgiveness, via the law of life, without understanding this requires abdication of ANY seat of judgment they have held in their own lives, including against themselves.

This tool is often helpful for those who feel they have been heard or given a voice in circumstances of betrayal, violation, abuse, and victimization. Two chairs are arranged facing each other: the individual takes one seat and using their creative imagination they are picturing the one needing to be released across from them. (They are not channeling or speaking to the other person in the spirit realm as some new age practices encourage, this is symbolic only.)

1) Begin by having them describe to the person (imagined) sitting across from them the debt that is owed and how it has impacted their life. For example: "You stole my innocence, you took advantage of our friendship, you manipulated me, etc..." Encourage specifics to be used here.

2) Follow this by describing the emotional impact this had. For example: "I began to fear being alone, or I thought I was dirty and without value."

3) Have the individual then declare that this debt is now between Jesus and the offender. Declaring out loud, addressing the person by name, that they release them to Jesus as the only Judge.

4) Have them, in their creative imagination, now picture the individual leaving the open chair before them and going to Jesus. Symbolically that individual is now in the custody of the Judge. In your creative imagination, now see Jesus sitting in that same seat in front of you.

5) Ask Holy Spirit if there is any unconfessed sin, false judgments or perspective adjustment the individual needs to personally repent of as a restful of the circumstances. If the individual has judged the value of the individual, not just the behavior that caused them pain, they are subject to the same judgment returning back onto themselves. For example: They deserve to die, never to be happy, they are unworthy of love, etc. Walk them through a time of repentance and listening as the Lord leads during this time.

For with the judgment you judge, you will be judged, and with the measure you use, it will be measured back to you. Matthew 7:2

6) Ask Jesus to now reveal how He sees that person. Have the individual finish by declaring out loud, as a sign of aligning their heart with the

Lord, what He says over the individual now in His custody.

7) Finish by making sure the individual feels a release of the bondage connected to the situation and has fully connected with the presence of the Lord in worship, adoration, with a sense of stability and peace. If anything still lingers, ask Holy Spirit what step needs to be more fully addressed.

Writing a Letter

If you do not feel comfortable walking through the Open Chair tool, you may consider writing a letter to the offender. Similar to the Open Chair, I encourage you to address the person by name and state the offense. Next, state how the offense has affected you and what emotions you have carried as a result. Write out how you have held judgment over them and repent of this and release them to the custody of Jesus. Write out a declaration of how Jesus sees that person and write out your agreement with this assessment of the individual. Write out, "(Offender's name), I forgive you of (insert the offense). I release you from my judgment and into the custody of Jesus Christ. I recognize that you are a child of God, beloved by Him"

I also encourage you to enter a time of prayer over the offender. Declare blessings over them. This is not a time to tell God how to deal with them. Genuinely move into a time of heartfelt pray for blessings for this individual, aligning your heart with the Father's heart of how He sees them.

Meeting with an Unbiased Party

At times a one-on-one meeting with the individual may be too difficult or unstable. It may be necessary to have an unbiased person sit-in with the two of you and guide the meeting. I highly recommend seeking a pastor, a counselor, or a person trained in inner healing and deliverance ministry. Perhaps it will be necessary to go through some sessions individually with the neutral party prior to a mixed meeting with one another. Keep in mind that with each of these tools the ultimate goal is always reconciliation, not being proven right, or receiving vengeance. These tools are meant for those who are truly seeking reconciliation within a relationship.

A side note on gift-giving. Often there are times where you may feel led to give a gift to someone as a peace offering. Usually there is nothing wrong with this, as long as it is being done from the correct heart posture of love and reconciliation and not manipulation. If you think there is any chance that you are attempting to win the person over by giving them a gift, this is manipulation. Manipulation is a tool of the kingdom of darkness and we are not trying to partner with Satan. If you are unsure, I would advise you to withhold on giving a gift until you feel a peace about it or that Holy Spirit has confirmed for you that is alright. We never want to manipulate someone into forgiveness or reconciliation. It must be a genuine desire of all parties involved. It may be best to hold out on giving a gift until after reconciliation has occurred.

I pray that as you have read through this book that your heart has been pierced by the Lord and that if there are any broken relationships, whether between you and the Father or between you and another person, that you seek reconciliation as soon as possible. I pray that as you walk with the Lord and get to know His heart that your heart begins to align with His. I pray that you begin to have a desire to carry the message of reconciliation that He has called us to carry. May the Lord go with you in peace and anoint your heart with unconditional love, grace and mercy. God bless you.

RECOMMENDED READING

Experiencing God Workbook: Knowing and Doing the Will of God
by: Henry T. Blackaby, Richard Blackaby, and Claude V. King

Compelled by Love
by: Heide Baker

That Incredible Christian
by: A.W. Towzer

The Bait of Satan
By: John Bevere

Waiting for His Heart
By: Joy McClain

Boundaries: When to say Yes, How to Say No, To Take Control of Your Life
By: Dr. Henry Cloud and Dr. John Townsend

Holy Spirit: The One Who Makes Jesus Real
By: Michael Koulianos

DESCRIPTION

Are you a murderer? Are you living a homosexual lifestyle? Have you had sex outside of marriage? Have you had an abortion? Are you addicted to drugs or alcohol? Are you a workaholic? Have you cheated on your spouse? Is it hard for you to imagine that any god could forgive your past? No matter what sin you have committed God loves you and desires to be reconciled to you.

Love to Reconcile reveals:
- The heart of the Father for His children.
- How we can receive forgiveness from God
- How our personal relationship can be healed through reconciliation.

If any of your relationships are strained, this book is for you! If you feel distant from God, this book is for you! If you are breathing, this book is for you!

REVIEW

Ann Lindholm, has called us to a higher standard in following God's plan of reconciliation through Love to Reconcile.

Ann is clearly saturated by the word of God, she is able to clearly communicate truth using the great examples of fallible human beings of the bible being reconciled to an infallible God.

Tammy Lane-President
www.Capernaumstudios.com
Executive Producer/Director

www.ingramcontent.com/pod-product-compliance
Lightning Source LLC
Chambersburg PA
CBHW051407290426
44108CB00015B/2192